Joel's Tunes

Joel's Tunes

Music and Text by
Joel Forrester

Cover Image: "Retro-Selfie of Dr. Real"
(Photograph by Joel Forrester, 1975)

An Evergreen Book

New York
2015

For Mary

Contents

ACKNOWLEDGMENTS

ratitude to Donald Elfman and Tony Bly and Matthew Garrity and too many others easily to mention.

INTRODUCTION

Welcome to an approximate one-fortieth of my compositional output.   I'm tempted to picture you. I won't try; but I wish you every success in making these tunes *your own!*

As a melodist and a partisan of melodic composition, I tried to choose pieces which tend to announce themselves, that leave neither the player nor the listener in any doubt as to their form or their progress. (I also chose from among the least messy of the lot.)

If heard chronologically, a picture might be developed of my 40 years in New York...but I doubt it: I've always maintained the practice of jotting down the first stirrings of a melody, the moment it crosses my mind, then working out its implications at the keyboard; and I've always composed, indiscriminately, out of the six categories suggested here.

But it is true that music from my early years in New York will be under-represented in this selection. Those were days when---driving a truck, painting an apartment, or doing the laundry of an animal hospital---I felt myself a Charles Ives *manqué* and my compositions rivaled my model's in austerity if in no other way. But then I started getting gigs and I found myself writing music for these gigs.

And when I found my mates ("mine own wild kind" as Pound put it), I wrote music for them and me to play together. Bassist David Hofstra freed my left hand for less-cluttered ensemble music. Drummer Denis Charles gave me so much of his sensed time that my own time is never in doubt. And Phillip Johnston gave me the voice of the saxophone as my primary conveyor of melody. I can hear all three of these guys in my head, any time I compose.

But the larger point is this: these 56 tunes were written in order to be *played*, and that's why I chose them to be published. I can imagine no happier afterlife than one in which my tunes are being played and enjoyed.

Would you try your hand? [Of course, I wouldn't mind, Twainishly, being allowed to observe that afterlife, myself.]

In each category, I try first to give the listener an idea of what I mean by what's comprehended there.   In a second paragraph, I offer the player clues to performance.

Musicians of my generation came of age in a time of promise, a time when it felt natural to keep freedom in mind.   It's my hope---nay, my belief---that these tunes encode something of the consciousness from which they emerged.

— JOEL FORRESTER, *New York,* 2015

Joel's Tunes

I. BLUES / Intro

It is a commonplace to locate the heart of jazz in the blues. But each new way of playing jazz must remind itself of the fact. And the blues, in its own heart of hearts, is a direct expression of the desire to escape the conditional nature of existence: none of us gets out alive and she knows it. Pain and loss in life serve as reminders of our larger condition, our "life sentence". Most of us cannot face these reminders with any regularity. Happily, the 20th Century was blessed with any number of women and men driven to inhabit this dilemma and not to get lost in it before finding a way to talk about it, to speak from the heart. I am not one of these, am rather a maker of blues-forms for myself and others to pour their feelings into. The blues tunes selected here, then, are empty houses. But I've decorated the walls.

What's true with jazz in general is true most imperatively with the blues: play these tunes in the radiance (or penumbra) of whatever you happen to be feeling at the moment. Make my blues a vehicle for your own; make them personal; render me inaudible.

Contents
Blue Tunes

Peggy's Blues

Joel Forrester

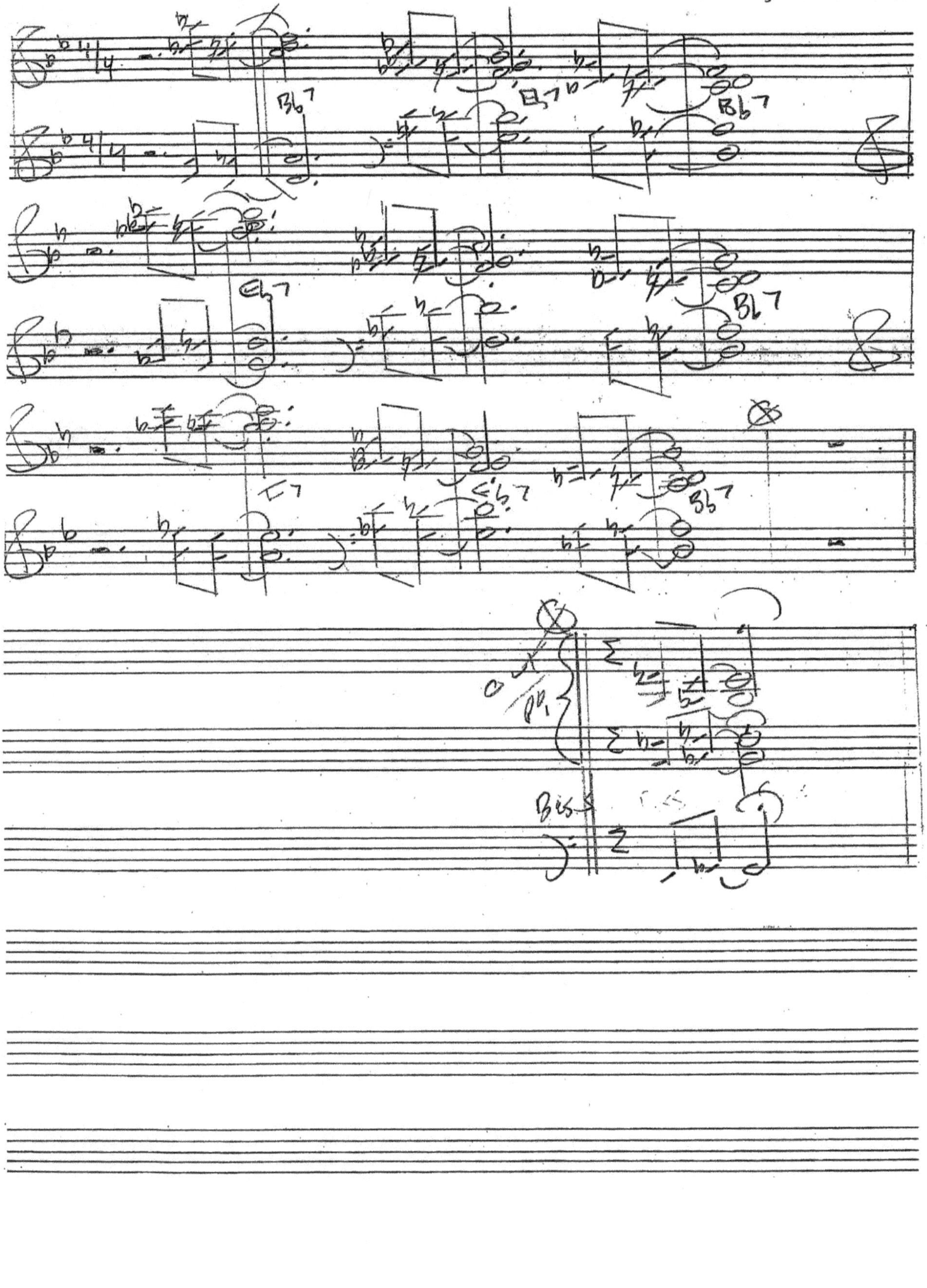

G. G.'s Blues

Joel Forrester

Blue Mary Lou

Joel Forrester

Flip Flop

Joel Forrester

White Blues

Joel Forrester

Loser's Blues

Joel Forrester

The Dave

Joel Forrester

II. BOP / Intro

The first bop I heard --- at age 10 --- was Thelonious Monk's and his is yet --- 60 years on --- the clearest imprint, the weirdest groove. The beboppers were heroic Moderns. Musicians today struggle to regain the foreground; business culture would force us into the role of providing appropriate background to other people's dramas. But bop's snap, its taste!, may still be accessed by willing ears. It still presents itself, unashamed, as a music that reeks of destiny. And Thelonious Monk is *still* weird!

Play my bop tunes at whatever tempo seems to suit but make sure they swing!   Hear a walking bass line (metered quarter notes) moving through these structures as you play them. Or, better, write out the chords for a bass player and invite him/her to play the tunes with you.

Contents
Bop Tunes

I Know What Girls Like

Joel Forrester

After You, Joel!

Joel Forrester

Sharpturn

Joel Forrester

The Bubble

Joel Forrester

solo chords on page 2.

The Bubble

(continued)

Joel Forrester

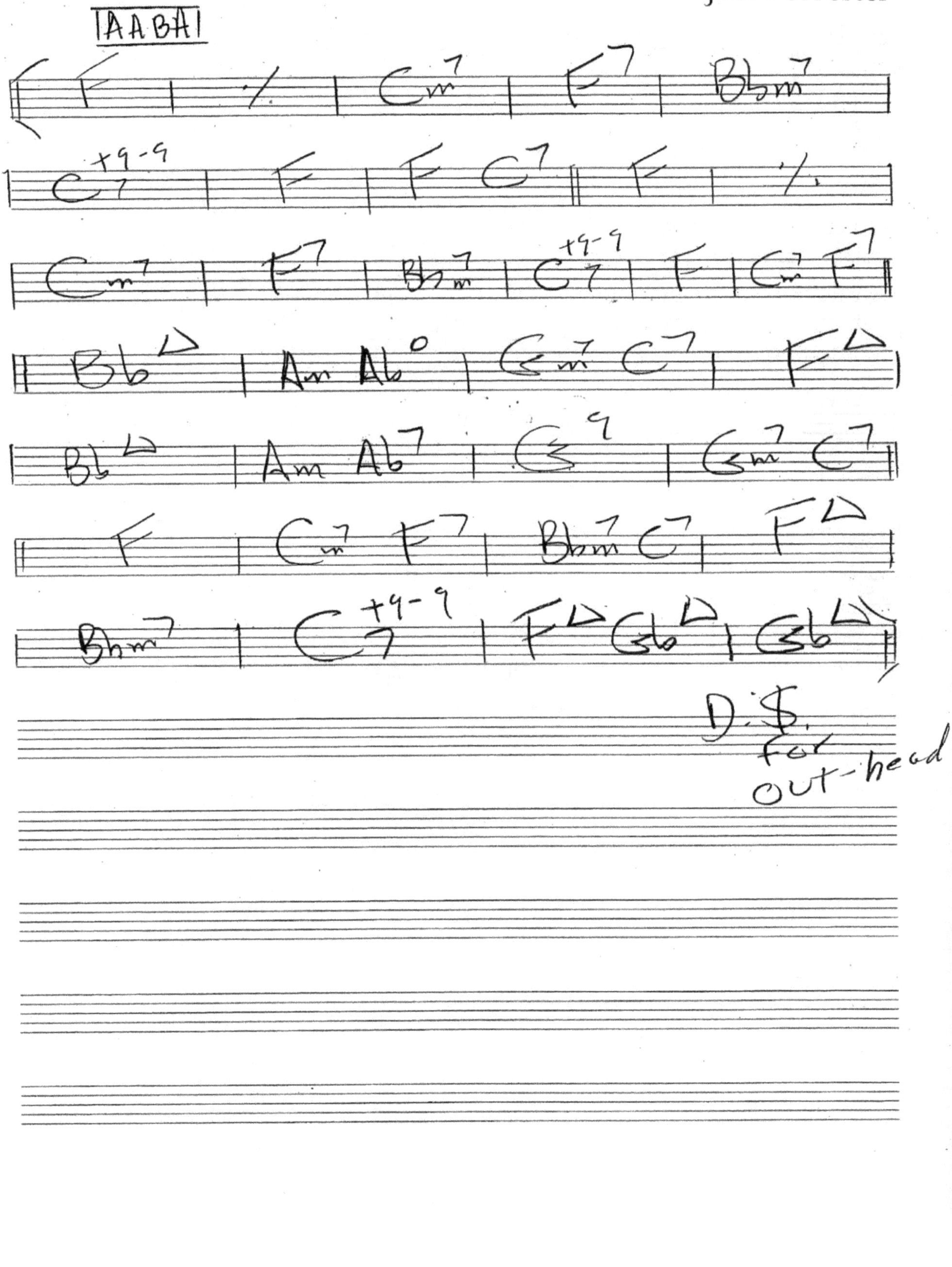

As If You Were

Joel Forrester

Don't Ask Me Now

aka "Karen 'n Ray"

Joel Forrester

I Believe It!

Joel Forrester

Your Bop Clock

Joel Forrester

Your Bop Clock

(continued)

Joel Forrester

Not Like That

Joel Forrester

What You Mean To Me

Joel Forrester

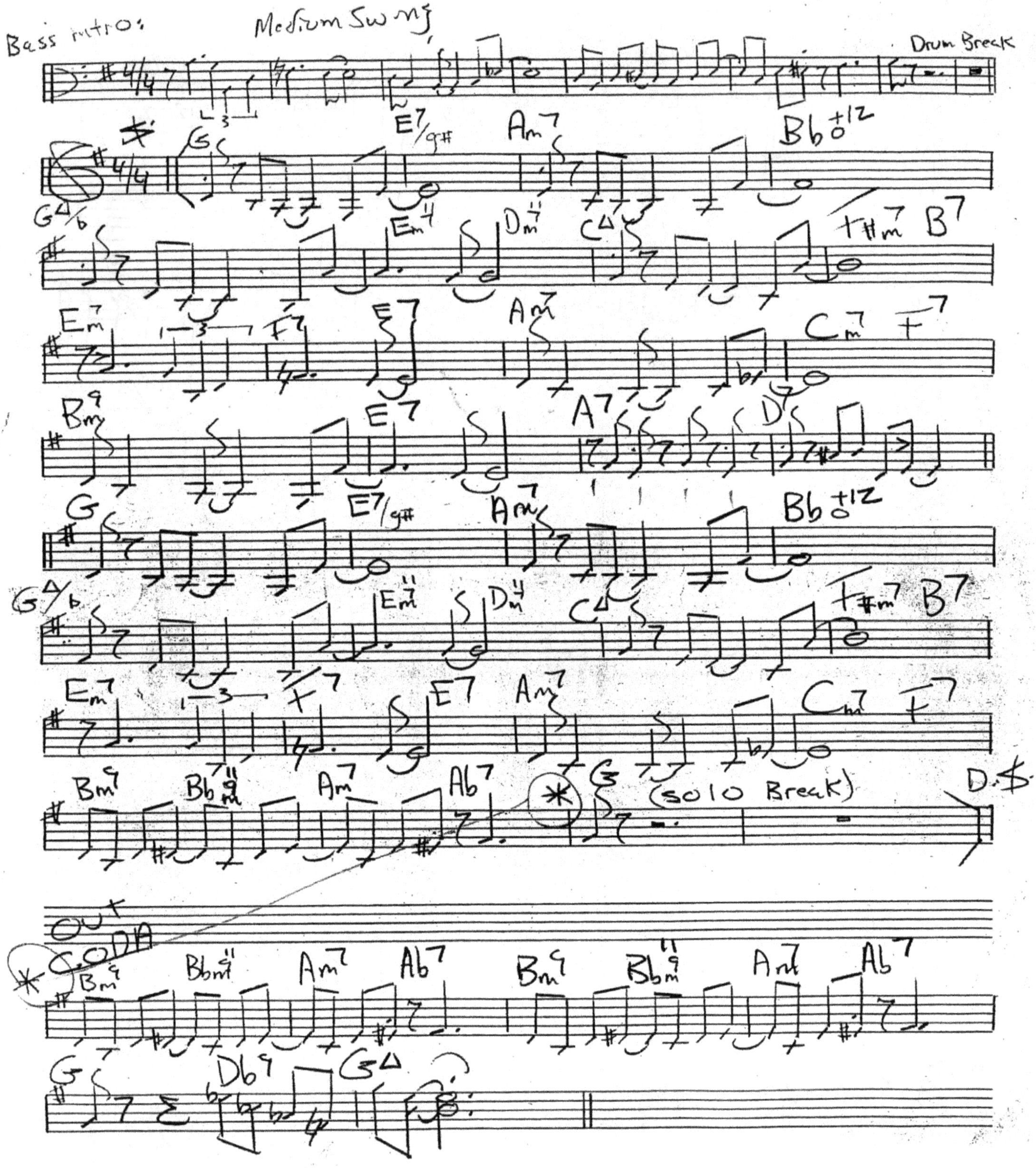

In Time

Joel Forrester

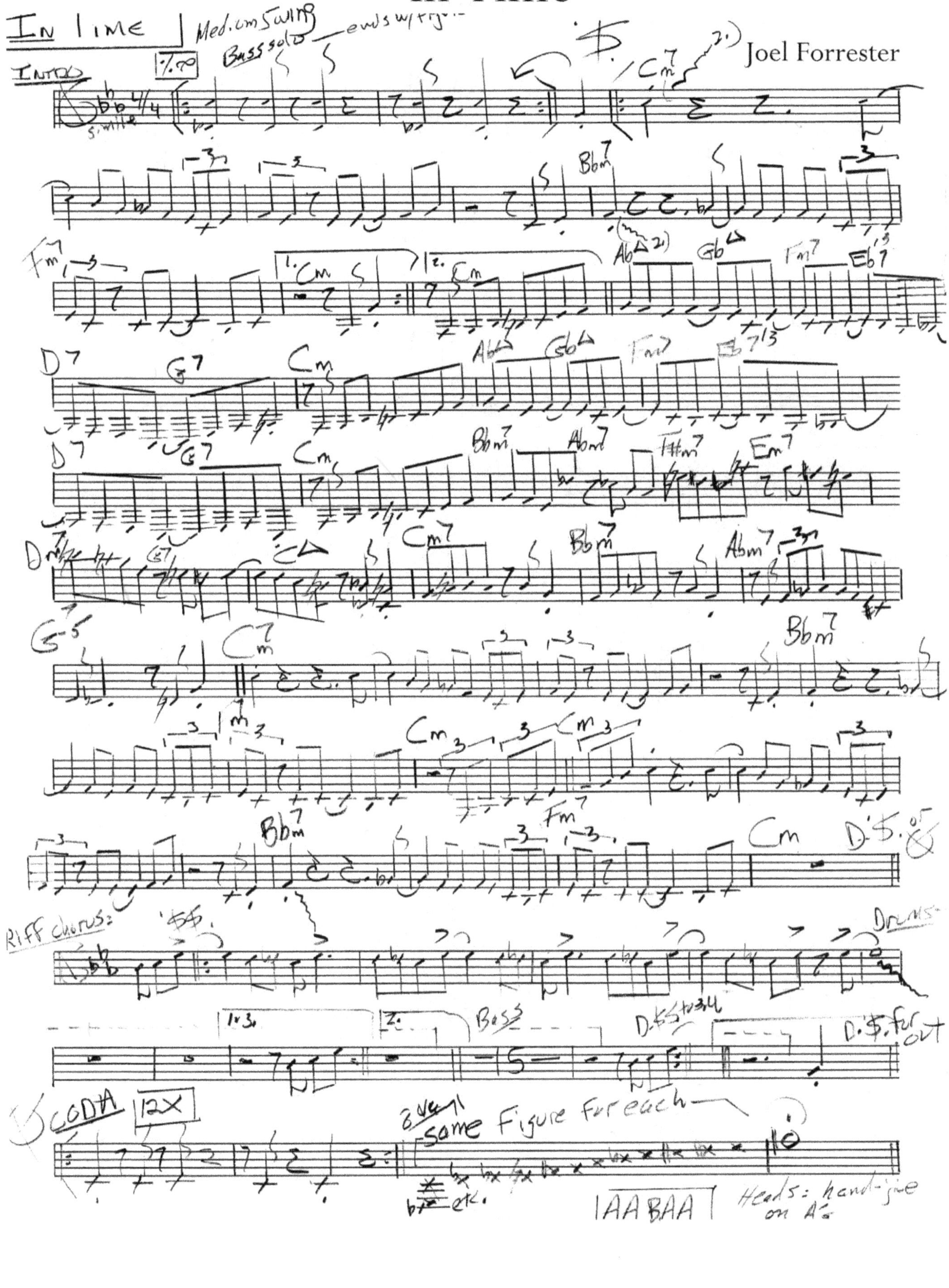

No Question

Joel Forrester

Medium Swing / Break tune

338.   1.

No Question
(continued)

Joel Forrester

No Question

(continued)

Joel Forrester

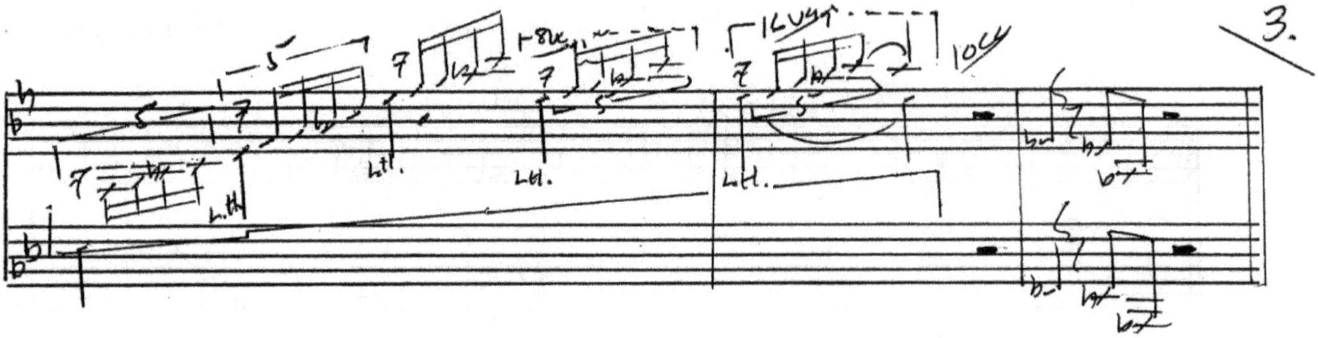

Sharkey Is Here!

Joel Forrester

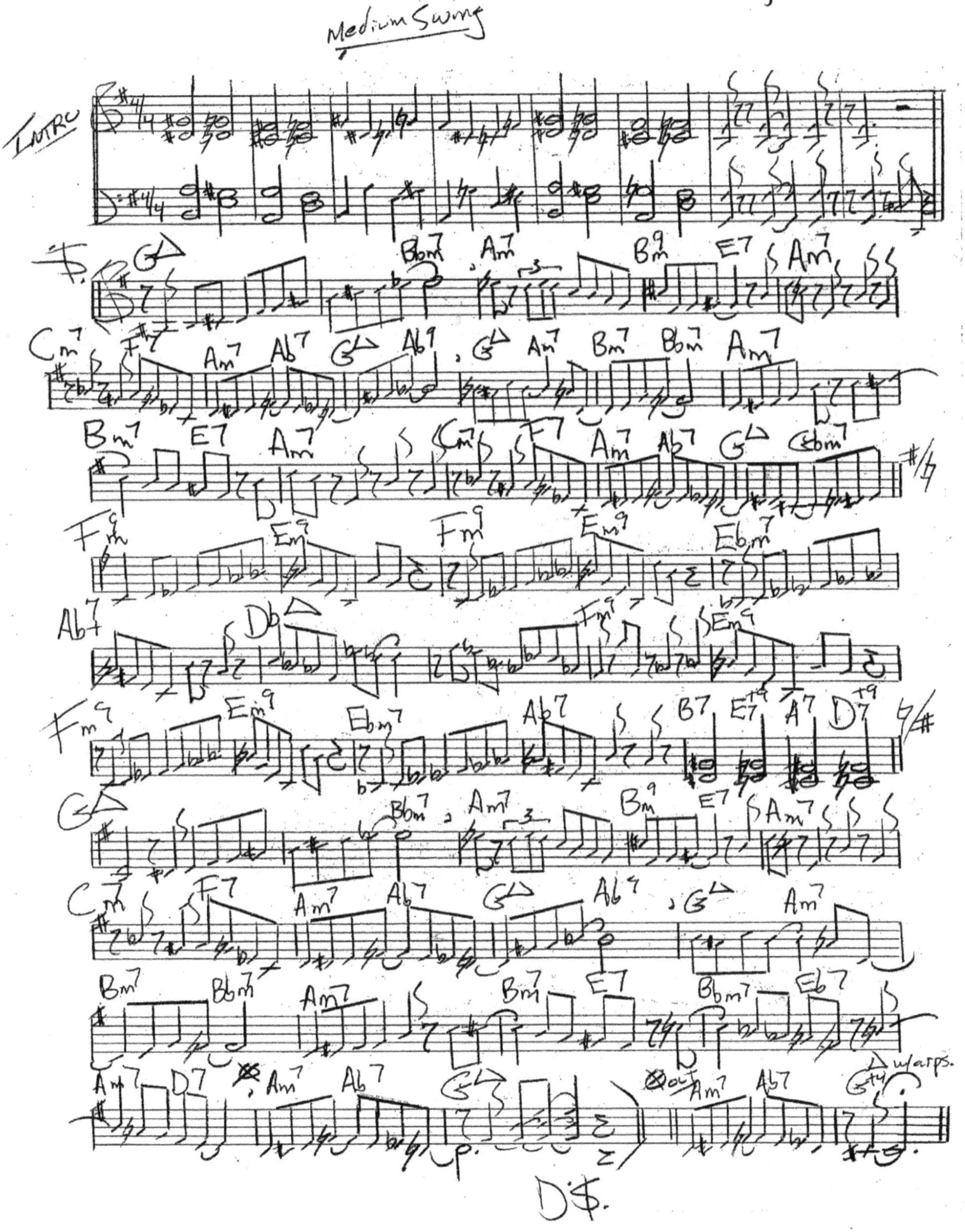

Nerve

Joel Forrester

N.B.: last 6 bars as INTRO

Wait For The Word

Joel Forreter

True

Joel Forreter

4.

What She Does

Joel Forrester

Mix-Up

Joel Forrester

Up Too Early

Joel Forrester

III. BALLADS / Intro

The ballad is the jazz form at the farthest remove from any species of dance music. Because of this, it presents the temptation to become ruminative, to sentimentalize. But in the strongest jazz ballads there is no need to substitute "feelings" for what is felt: the melody and its attendant harmony lead the ear into a depth available nowhere else. (I exaggerate but not unduly.)

Play these ballads as slowly as you can while keeping the time. The more space you can conjure --- without losing the time --- the better! And try to limit your use of the sustain pedal. Pedaling ought never to blur melody, unless you want it to.

Contents
Ballad Tunes

About Francoise

Joel Forrester

Your Little Dog

Joel Forrester

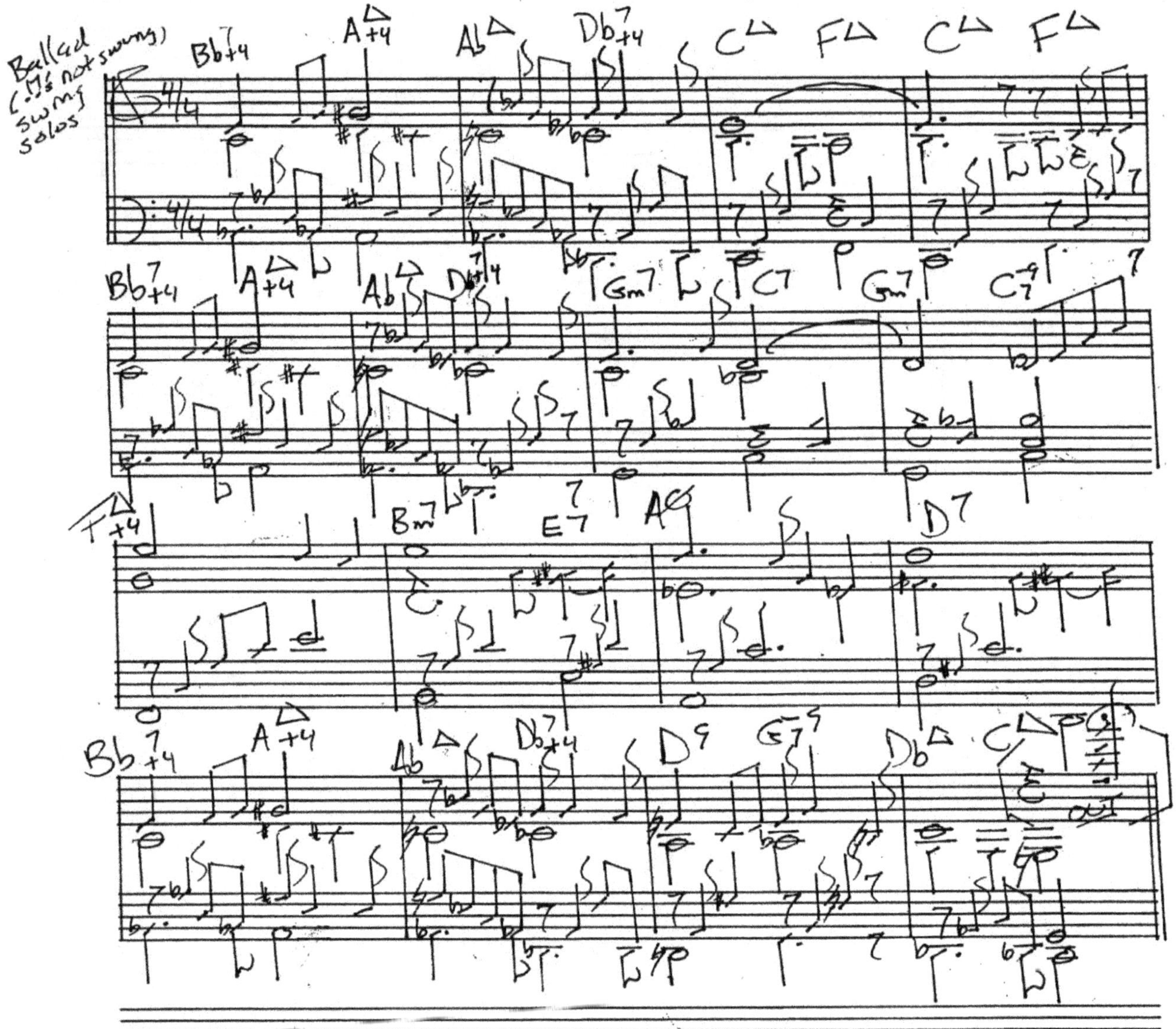

When I Was In Heaven

Joel Forrester

Nothing Lasts Forever

Joel Forrester

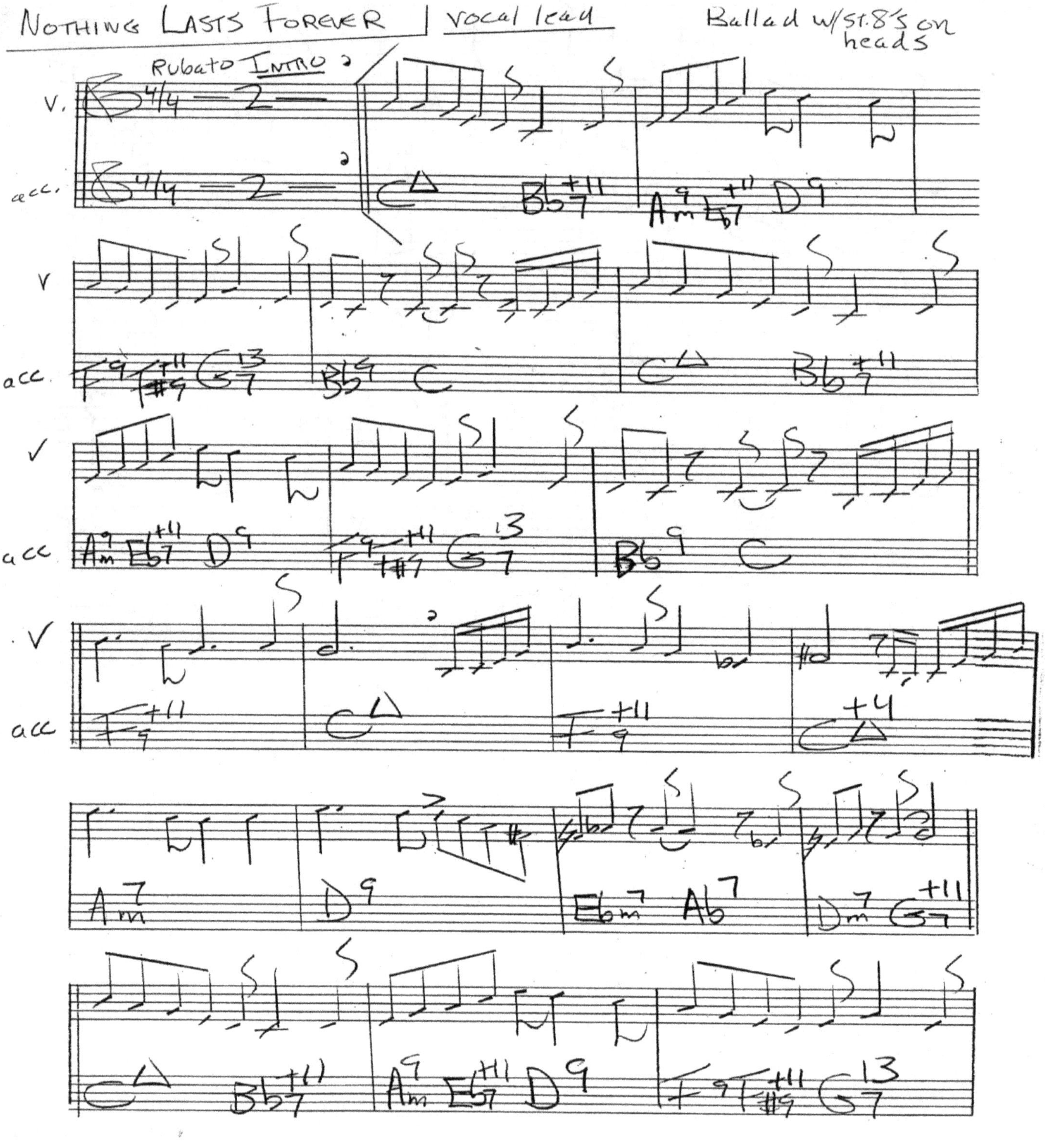

Nothing Lasts Forever
(continued)

Joel Forrester

Living In The World

Joel Forrester

Serenade

Joel Forrester

Gone Tomorrow

Joel Forrester

SLOW BALLAD FEEL
HEADS DON'T SWING/SOLOS DO

Gone Tomorrow
(continued)

Joel Forrester

IV. SALON / Intro

The composer thanks the cellist David Preiser for titling this category.   These tunes are pianistic and encourage interpretation rather than improvising. But, as with certain "serious" pieces of Gershwin's, they are best realized when left in the hands of a jazz musician.

I suggest that the pianist follow Monk's dictum: employ marked tempo shifts rather than *rubato*. "Imaginary Paris" should project a sense of anticipation. The trio of properly Parisian tunes are --- in mood and harmony --- all of a piece; I try to follow Preiser's suggestion that performance point up distinctions among them.   In "The Visit", it's important to tease out the melody; it should be one sinuous line.

Contents
Salon Tunes

The Visit

Joel Forrester

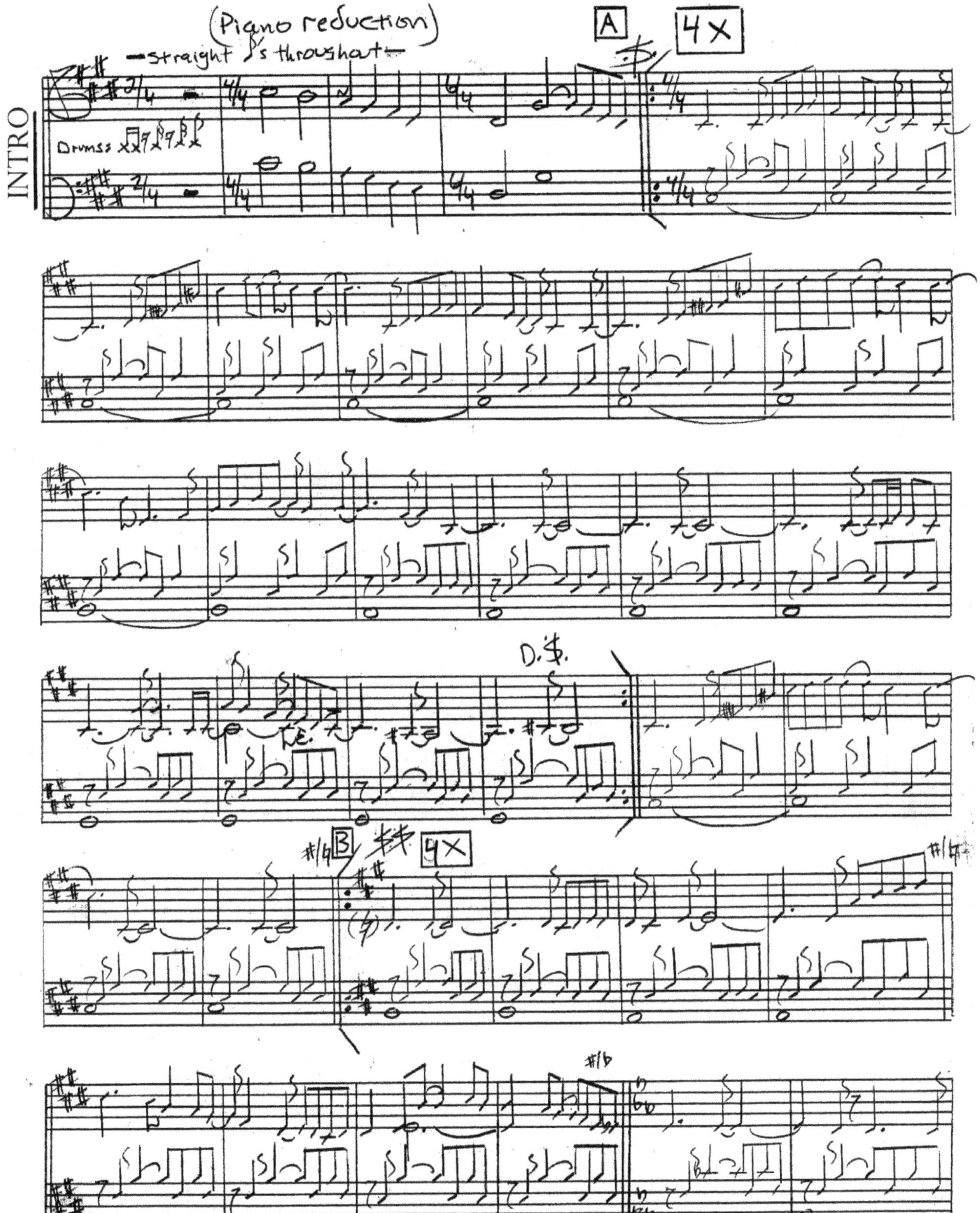

The Visit
(continued 2)

Joel Forrester

ON TO P.3

The Visit
(continued 3)

Joel Forrester

Drunk Bach

Joel Forrester

Drunk Bach
(continued)

Joel Forrester

Manuscript paper from Take Note Publishing Ltd www.takenote.co.uk

Imaginary Paris

Joel Forrester

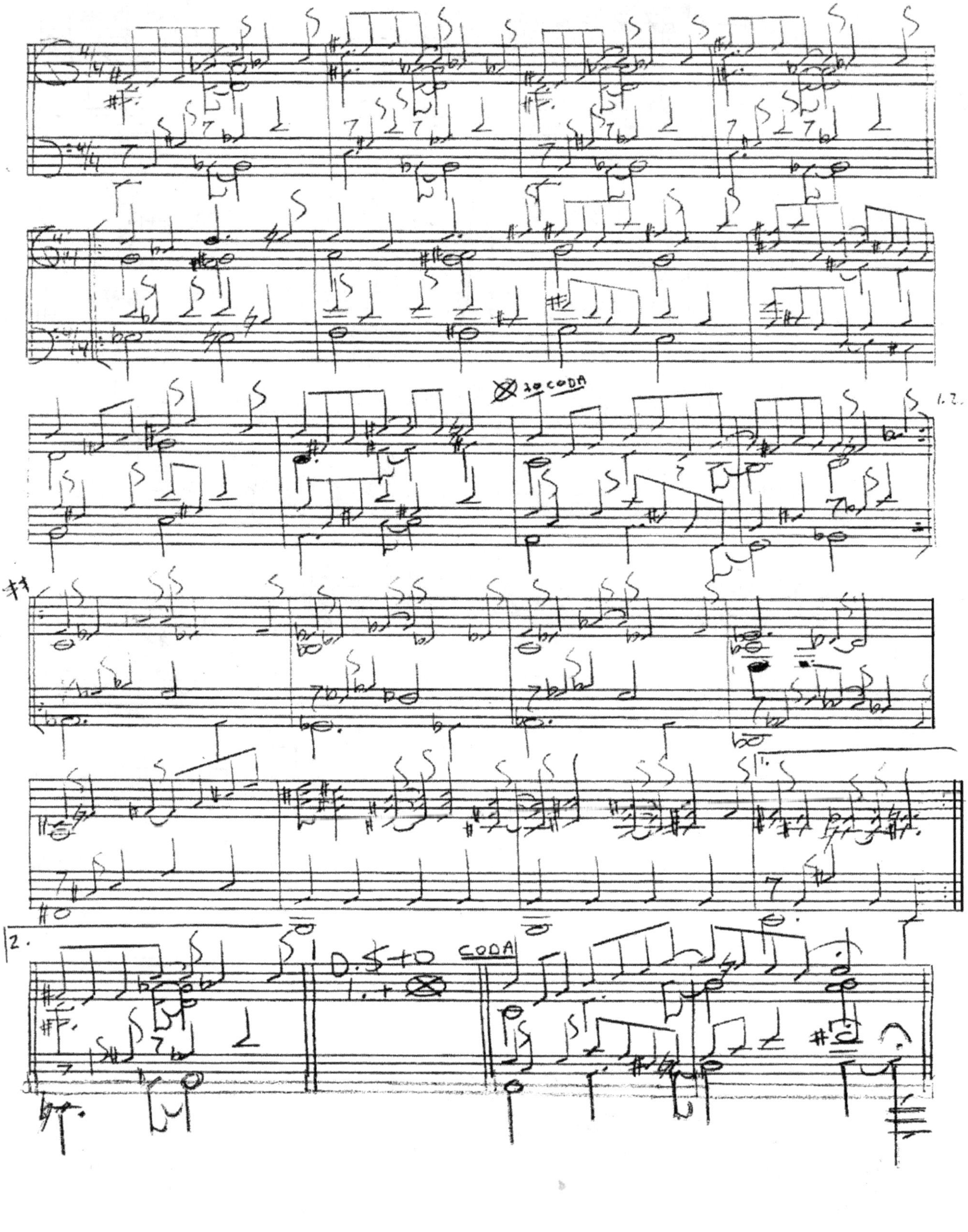

Turnings

Joel Forrester

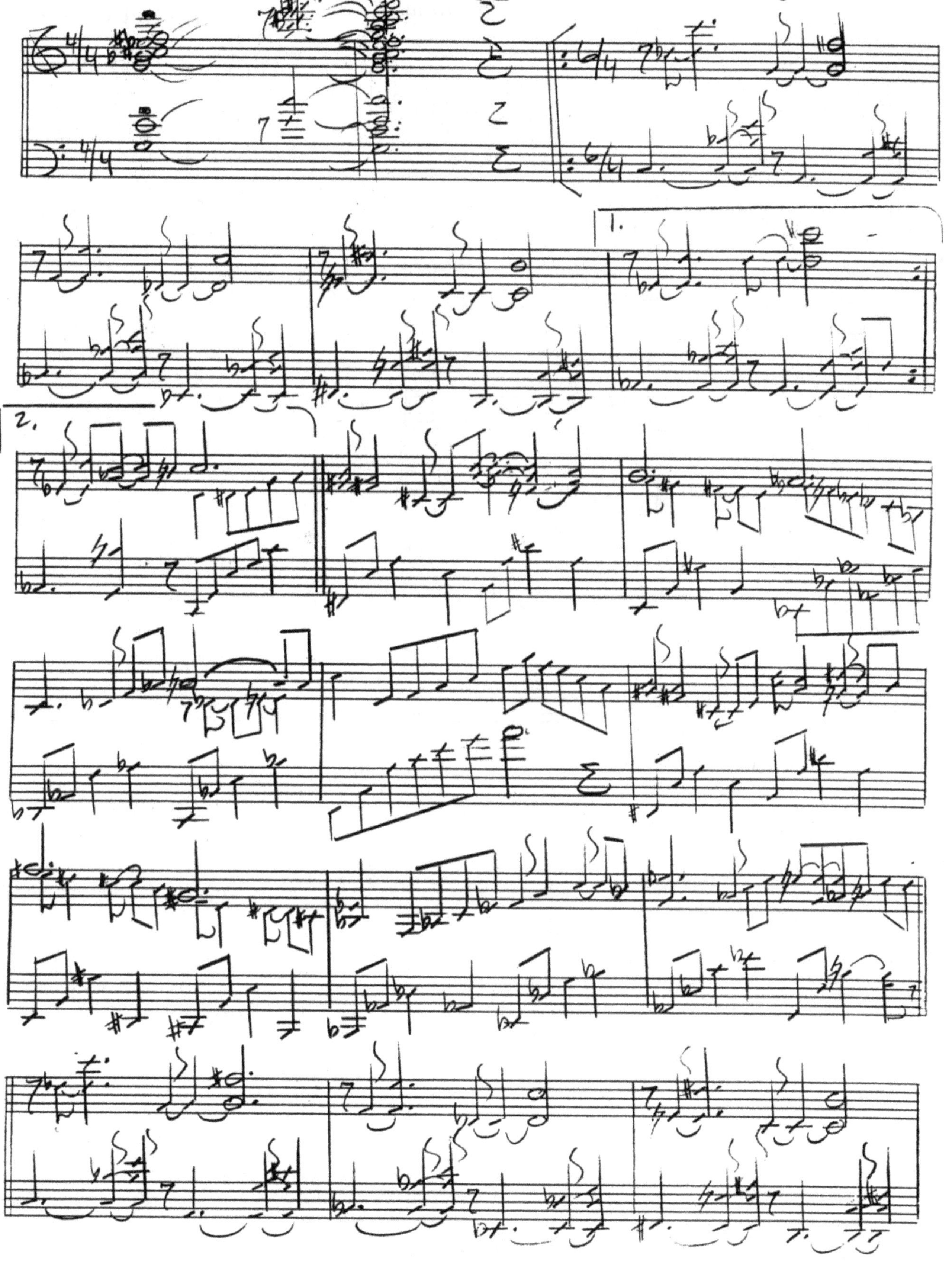

Turnings
(continued)

Joel Forrester

Il Pleut

Joel Forrester

Skies Of Paris

Joel Forrester

Skies Of Paris

(continued 2)

Joel Forrester

Skies Of Paris
(continued 3)

Joel Forrester

V. 2 - BEAT / Intro

I've written hundreds of tunes that might belong here; in the animated cartoon of my life, they jostle for inclusion. (I've included one because it's been recorded and the other because it hasn't.) One master-narrative of the development of jazz explains its "progress" by looking to the composers---usually pianists!---who took the ensemble music of their day and re-fashioned it as piano music (from which state it was, often, re-programmed to the ensembles of tomorrow); Morton and Joplin, of course; but also Hines, Ellington, then Monk and Nichols...and yes even Cecil Taylor. Their game-changing grandeur is not mine; but stride and other two-beat forms have always allowed a pianist/composer to conjure a *complete* music.

The left hand needn't be emphasized; it already forms the bedrock of the music. A good listen to the stride- and ragtime-masters will indicate a more varied palette of left-hand colors than might be imagined. And, of course, the pianist is encouraged to discover her own sinister ways.

Contents
2 - Beat Tunes

Snugglebunnies

Joel Forrester

The Sperm Of The Moment

Joel Forrester

VI. Straight – 8ᵗʰs / Intro

This is a catch-all category for tunes of mine that do not swing; that is: whose eighth-note figures are not disguised triplets. "Stop", "Wonder", "Beautiful Girl", "Straight", and "K's" are all subspecial Latin tunes. (A composer cannot live in New York without its dominant rhythms taking root.) "Bunny" is a shuffle. "Monkey', "No Time", and "No Ghosts" are hybrids. "Your Political" and "Away" are would-be rock anthems.   "Get" puts a motor under a theme of Chopin's. "Just Like" is a come-all-ye. And "Second" is a brief example of my overtly-repetitive music.

In playing "Second Nature", the pianist should constantly vary accents in both hands, so that the 11's fall only intermittently into a groove. And the piece is too short to be allowed to lapse into a lull.

Contents
Straight – 8ths

No Time

Joel Forrester

No Time
(continued)

Joel Forrester

2nd Nature

Joel Forrester

2nd Nature

(continued)

Joel Forrester

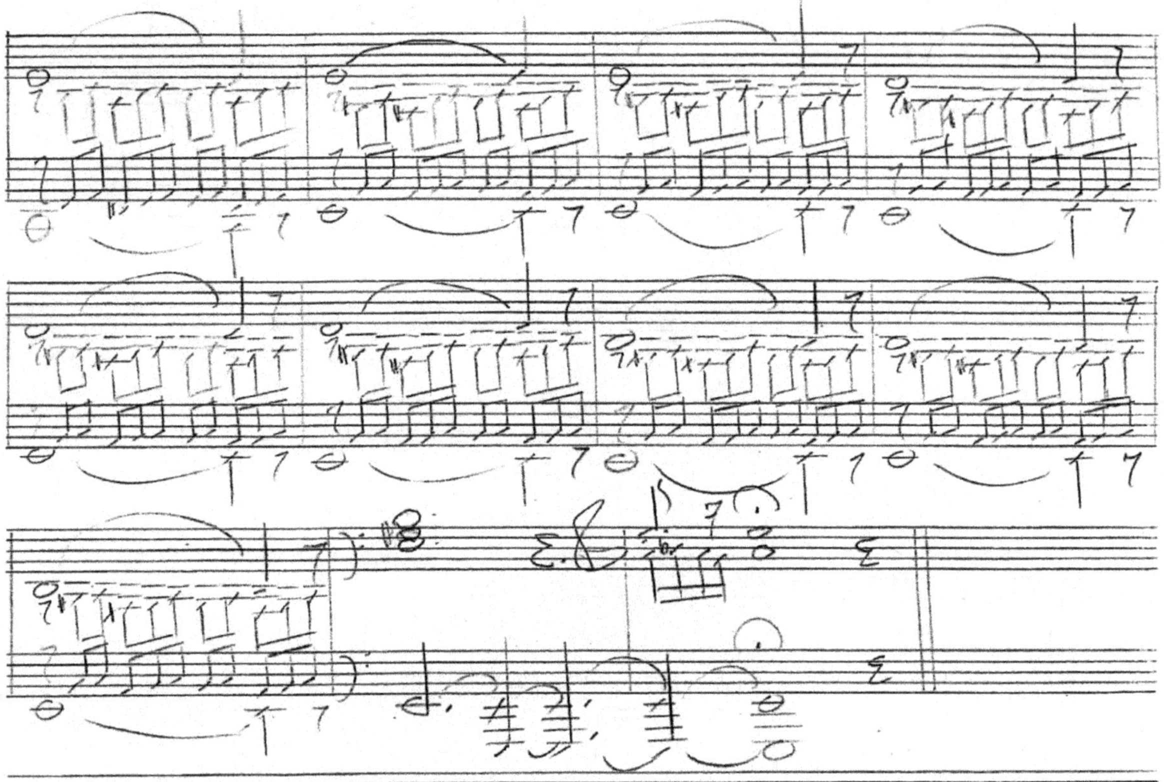

Stop the Music

Joel Forrester

Stop the Music

(continued)

Joel Forrester

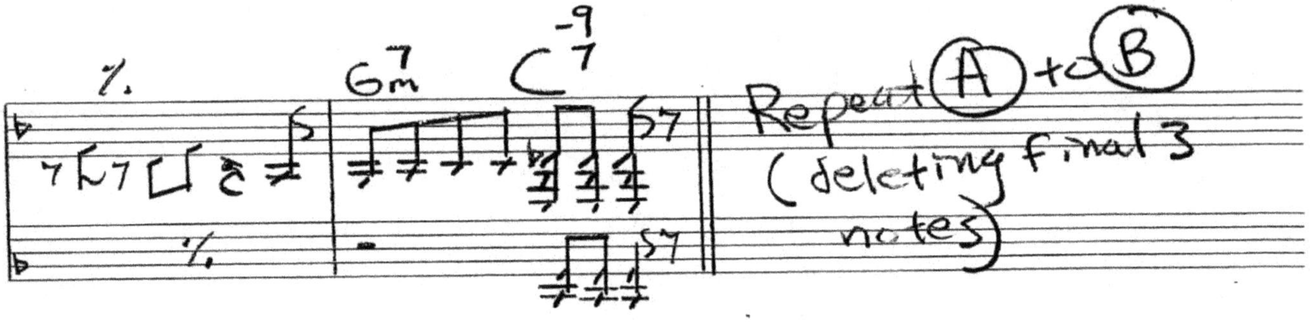

Your Political Movie

Joel Forrester

Your Political Movie
(continuted)

Joel Forrester

The Beautiful Girl in the Moon

Joel Forrester

Piano's 2nd solo chorus
has a 2-Bar break
before arranged - Ⓑ:
then Ⓒ is swung

The Beautiful Girl in the Moon

(continued)

Joel Forrester

Bunny Boy

Joel Forrester

Bunny Boy

(continued)

Joel Forrester

Monkey in the Middle

Joel Forrester

Straight Ahead

Joel Forrester

No Ghosts

Joel Forrester

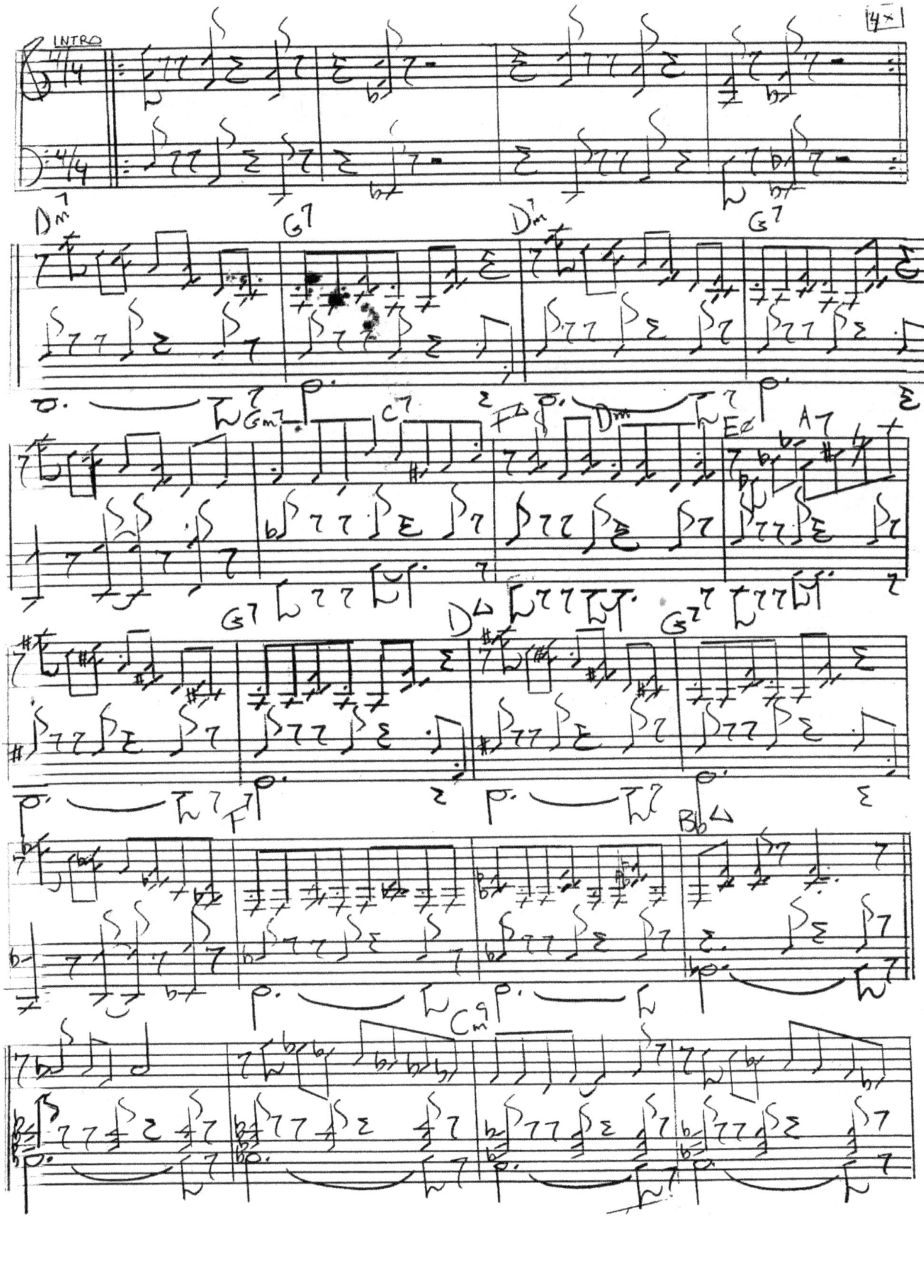

No Ghosts
(continued)

Joel Forrester

Just Like Him

Joel Forrester

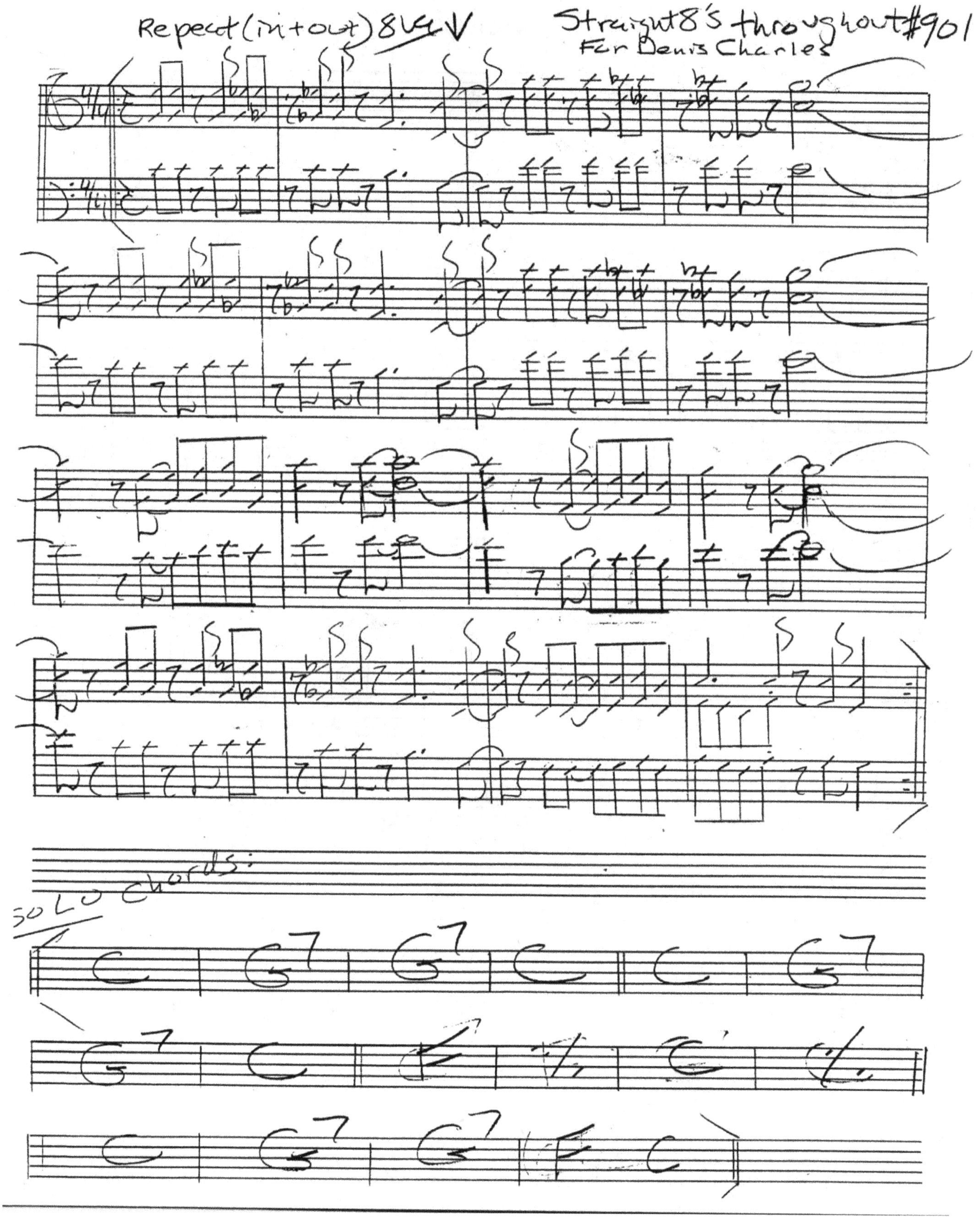

Skirmish

Joel Forrester

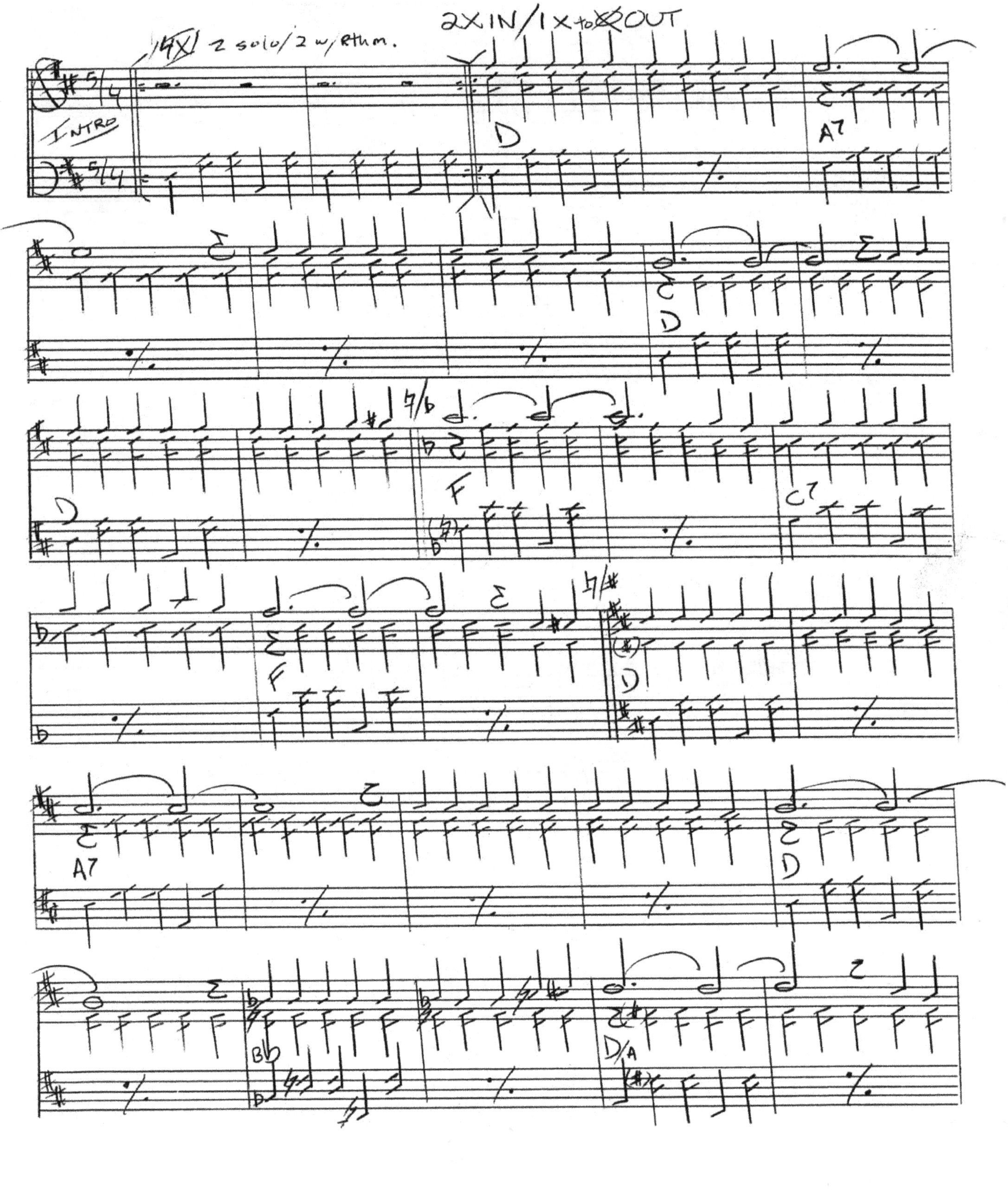

Skirmish
(continued)

Joel Forrester

Get Serious

Joel Forrester

Not swing
A
B
OUT:
3X
1. To B
2. D.C.
Solo Follows Form: ABB

Away

Joel Forrester

Kirsten's New Mambo

Joel Forrester

I Wonder

Joel Forrester

About the Author:

Joel Forrester is a stride and bop pianist, living and working in New York. He records for Donald Elfman's Ride Symbol label; his most recent release is THE LATE JOEL FORRESTER QUARTET (2015), which features Vito Dieterle on tenor sax. He gigs around town as a soloist and with small ensembles, performing pre-dominantly his own tunes. With Phillip Johnston, he continues to co-lead the Microscopic Septet. He also heads a quintet based in south-central France. He accompanies silent films for the American Academy of Motion Pictures Arts & Sciences. Among his nearly 2000 compositions are the theme to NPR's FRESH AIR WITH TERRY GROSS, the off-Broadway musical FASCIST LIVING, and the 8-hour piano piece INDUSTRIAL ARTS. Earlier in his life, Forrester received the criticism and encouragement of Thelonious Monk and Pannonica deKoenigswarter. As a pretentious young squirt, he supplied music for the early films of Andy Warhol. He has recently entered his eighth decade on earth.

www.ingramcontent.com/pod-product-compliance
Lightning Source LLC
Chambersburg PA
CBHW062111090426
42741CB00016B/3395